Question Time

Creepy-crawlies

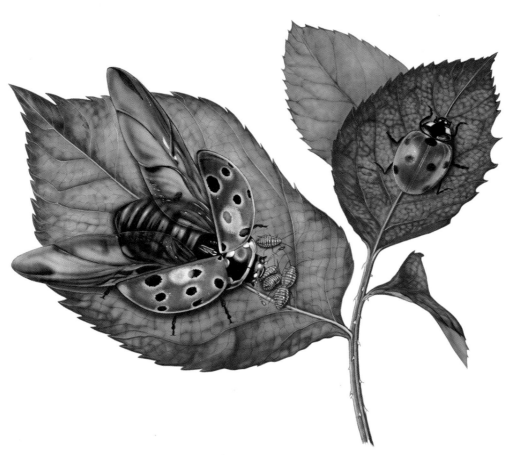

Jim Bruce

KING*f*ISHER

Editor: Emma Wild
Designer: Catherine Goldsmith
Consultants: Joyce Pope, Norah Granger
Indexer: Jason Hook
Production controller: Caroline Hansell
Illustrators: Lisa Alderson 10-11, 16-17, 22-23, 26-27;
Ray Grinaway 4-5, 12-13 28-29; Ian Jackson 8-9;
Joannah May 6-7, 20-21; Andrew Robinson 14-15.
Cartoons: Ian Dicks
Picture Manager: Jane Lambert
Picture acknowledgements:
7tl Kjell B. Sandved/www.osf.uk.com; 9tl Brian Bevan/Ardea
London; 15tl G.I. Bernard/www.osf.uk.com; 17tr R.J.Erwin/NHPA
1992; 18tr Harald Lange/Bruce Coleman Collection; 19tr Stephen
Dalton/NHPA; 21tl James Carmichael Jr./NHPA; 23tr Ron
Nunnington/www.osf.uk.com; 24tl Harald Lange/Bruce Coleman
Collection; 29tl Isaac Kehimkar/www.osf.uk.com.

Every effort has been made to trace the copyright holders of the photographs.
The publishers apologise for any inconvenience caused.

KINGFISHER
Kingfisher Publications Plc,
New Penderel House,
283–288 High Holborn,
London WC1V 7HZ
www.kingfisherpub.com

First published by Kingfisher Publications Plc 2001
10 9 8 7 6 5 4 3 2

2TR/0303/TIMS/RNB/128 MA

Copyright © Kingfisher Publications Plc 2001

All rights reserved. No part of this publication may be
reproduced, stored in a retrieval system or transmitted
by any means, electronic, mechanical, photocopying or
otherwise, without the prior permission of the publisher.

A CIP catalogue record for this book
is available from the British Library.

ISBN 0 7534 0627 6

Printed in China

CONTENTS

ABOUT this book

Have you ever wondered why honeybees like flowers? On every page, find out the answers to questions like this and other fascinating facts about creepy-crawlies. Words in **bold** are explained in the glossary on page 31.

Look and Find ★ ladybird ★

All through the book you will see the **Look and Find** symbol. This has the name and picture of a small object that is hidden somewhere on the page. Look carefully to see if you can find it.

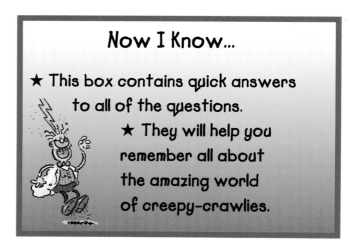

Now I Know...

★ This box contains quick answers to all of the questions.
★ They will help you remember all about the amazing world of creepy-crawlies.

★ Look and Find ★
caterpillar

WHAT are creepy-crawlies?

Creepy-crawlies are tiny creatures that buzz, scuttle, wriggle and creep all around us. Creepy-crawlies include **insects**, spiders, millipedes, worms, woodlice, slugs and snails. They vary in size, shape and colour, but they are all **invertebrates**. This means they have no backbone.

WHERE do they live?

Creepy-crawlies are found almost everywhere on Earth. Every garden is home to thousands of them. They are so small that they can squeeze into the tiniest of spaces and can be very hard to spot. Creepy-crawlies hide in dark, damp places, such as under stones, leaves and logs, and in the soil. Some are busy during the day, but others come out only at night.

HOW many creepy-crawlies are there?

There are more creepy-crawlies in the world than any other kind of animal – over three million **species**. In fact, there are so many different kinds that scientists have sorted them into groups. For example, bees, ants and dragonflies are insects, spiders and scorpions are **arachnids**, and snails and slugs are **molluscs**.

That's Amazing!

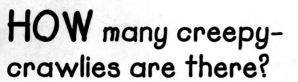

The first flight on Earth was not made by a bird, but by an insect – over 400 million years ago!

All sorts of creepy-crawlies are hiding in the long grass. Look out for them throughout the book.

Now I Know...

★ Creepy-crawlies are small creatures without backbones.
★ Creepy-crawlies live almost everywhere on Earth.
★ There are over three million kinds of creepy-crawly.

WHY do insects wear armour?

All insects have a hard casing on the outside of their body called an **exoskeleton**. Just like a strong suit of armour, this protects their soft insides. All insects have three parts to their bodies. The front part, the head, holds the brain, mouth, eyes and **antennae**. The middle part, the **thorax**, carries three pairs of legs and usually contains the wings. The back part, the **abdomen**, contains the stomach. In female insects, this is where the eggs are made.

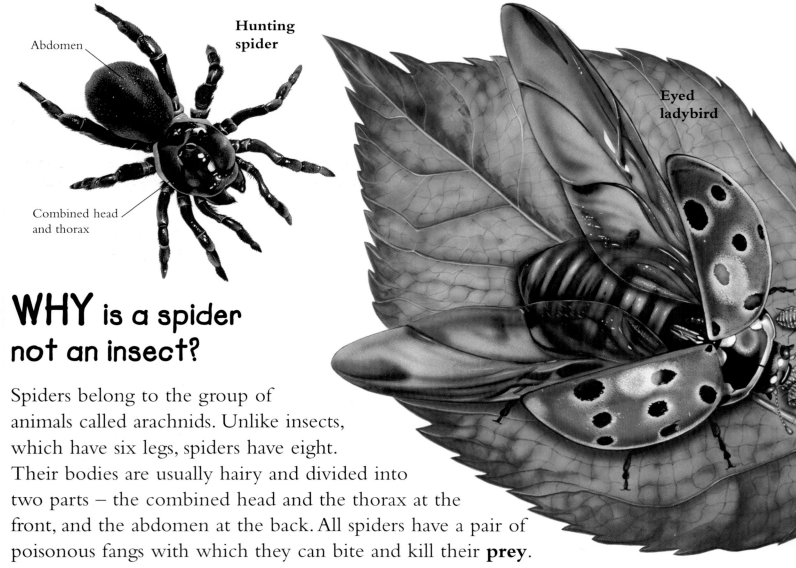

Abdomen

Hunting spider

Combined head and thorax

Eyed ladybird

WHY is a spider not an insect?

Spiders belong to the group of animals called arachnids. Unlike insects, which have six legs, spiders have eight. Their bodies are usually hairy and divided into two parts – the combined head and the thorax at the front, and the abdomen at the back. All spiders have a pair of poisonous fangs with which they can bite and kill their **prey**.

HOW do insects see?

Many animals have only one lens in each eye, but insects such as dragonflies and horse flies have **compound eyes**. Their eyes are made up of thousands of tiny lenses packed together. This kind of eye does not see objects clearly, but it does allow the insects to spot even the slightest movement from almost any direction.

That's Amazing!

When it is very cold, some insects produce special chemicals that stop their blood turning to ice!

Creepy-crawlies have different coloured blood to other animals – it is green or yellow!

Seven spot
ladybird

All creepy-crawlies, including ladybirds, have similar parts on the inside. They have nerves which carry signals from one part of their body to another, and they breathe using tiny air pipes called **tracheae**.

Now I Know...

★ All insects have an exoskeleton, three body parts and six legs.
★ Spiders have two body parts, eight legs and fangs.
★ An insect's eye is packed with thousands of tiny lenses.

WHY do grasshoppers lose their skin?

Female grasshoppers lay eggs. The newborn insects that hatch out are called **nymphs**. They look like tiny copies of their parents, but without wings. Grasshoppers grow in stages. As the nymphs grow bigger, their outer skin becomes too small and they wriggle out. This is called **moulting**. The insects then grow before their new skin hardens.

HOW many eggs do insects lay?

Female grasshoppers lay as few as two, or as many as 120 eggs at a time, though some insects can lay thousands. Egg shells keep the young warm, moist and hidden. Insects often leave their eggs on or near food that the young insects will eat after they hatch.

Female grasshoppers often lay their eggs in sandy soil. After they hatch, the young grasshoppers dig their way out to the surface.

Young grasshopper

Grasshopper eggs

Grasshopper nymph

One kind of grasshopper, called a locust, can gather in huge groups of up to 250,000 million insects!

WHAT grows in a bag?

To keep their babies safe, some spiders wrap their eggs in a home-made silk bag called a sac. Some hang this sac on their webs, while others carry it around on their backs. Young spiders, called **spiderlings**, hatch inside the egg sac. They leave after their first moult, when they are able to spin silk.

Old skin

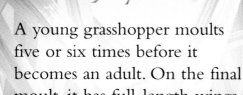

Final moult

A young grasshopper moults five or six times before it becomes an adult. On the final moult, it has full-length wings.

Now I Know...

★ When they are born, grasshoppers look like tiny copies of their parents.
★ Most insects lay a lot of eggs usually near a food source.
★ Some spiders wrap their eggs in a silk bag called a sac.

Look and Find ladybird

HOW do caterpillars grow up?

A wriggling caterpillar and a colourful, fluttering butterfly look very different. In fact, they are actually the same insect at different stages of life. Every young caterpillar will change its shape, size and colour before it becomes an adult butterfly. This is called **metamorphosis**.

1 Female butterflies lay eggs on plants that will provide the young caterpillars with the type of food they eat.

2 When the eggs hatch, the caterpillars immediately start to eat and grow quickly.

3 When fully grown, the caterpillars become **pupae**. They make a special shell in which their bodies begin to change.

4 After some time, the shell splits open and a new adult butterfly wriggles free.

A swallowtail caterpillar feeding

That's Amazing!

Some fully-grown caterpillars can weigh up to 2,700 times more than they did at birth!

Thirsty butterflies sip the juice of rotten fruit that contains alcohol!

Although most caterpillars have twelve eyes, their eyesight is still very poor. They can only tell the difference between light and dark. Some caterpillars have no eyes at all, and get around by using touch and smell alone.

WHAT do butterflies eat?

Adult butterflies do not need much food, but they do need sugars, such as **nectar**, for energy. Brightly-coloured flowers contain this liquid. The butterflies unroll their long tongues, and suck up sticky nectar from inside the flowers. When they are thirsty, they drink water from ponds and streams.

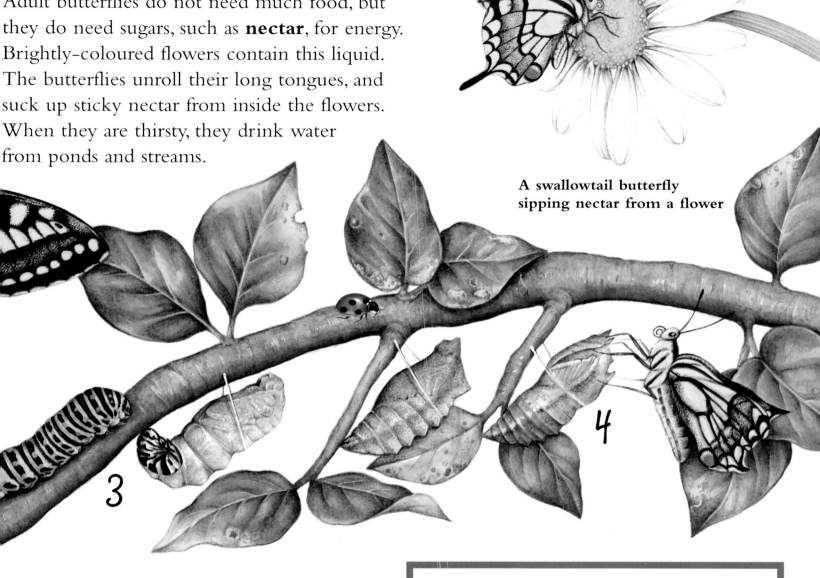

A swallowtail butterfly sipping nectar from a flower

3

4

WHERE do butterflies go to sleep?

At night-time and in bad weather, butterflies find a quiet place to sleep, on the underside of twigs and leaves, or on the top of a blade of grass. They often rest in the same place night after night.

Now I Know...

★ Caterpillars change a lot before they become butterflies.
★ Nectar is a sweet, sticky fluid that butterflies eat.
★ Butterflies often sleep in the same place every night.

WHAT do creepy-crawlies eat?

The dark woodland floor is an ideal place for creepy-crawlies, providing food and shelter. There are plenty of plants to nibble on or hide under, and lots of tiny animals to catch. Worms, snails, millipedes and woodlice feed on the rotting remains of plants as well as leaves, fruits and seeds. In turn, these plant-eating creepy-crawlies are food for ferocious woodland hunters such as spiders and beetles.

WHY do stag beetles have big jaws?

Many beetles have powerful jaws for grabbing, biting and chewing their prey. Male stag beetles have large jaws shaped like a pair of antlers. During the breeding season, they use them to wrestle with rival males, sometimes lifting them off the ground.

Plant-eaters and hunters feeding

Male stag beetles

Millipede

Millipede

Earthworm

Woodlouse

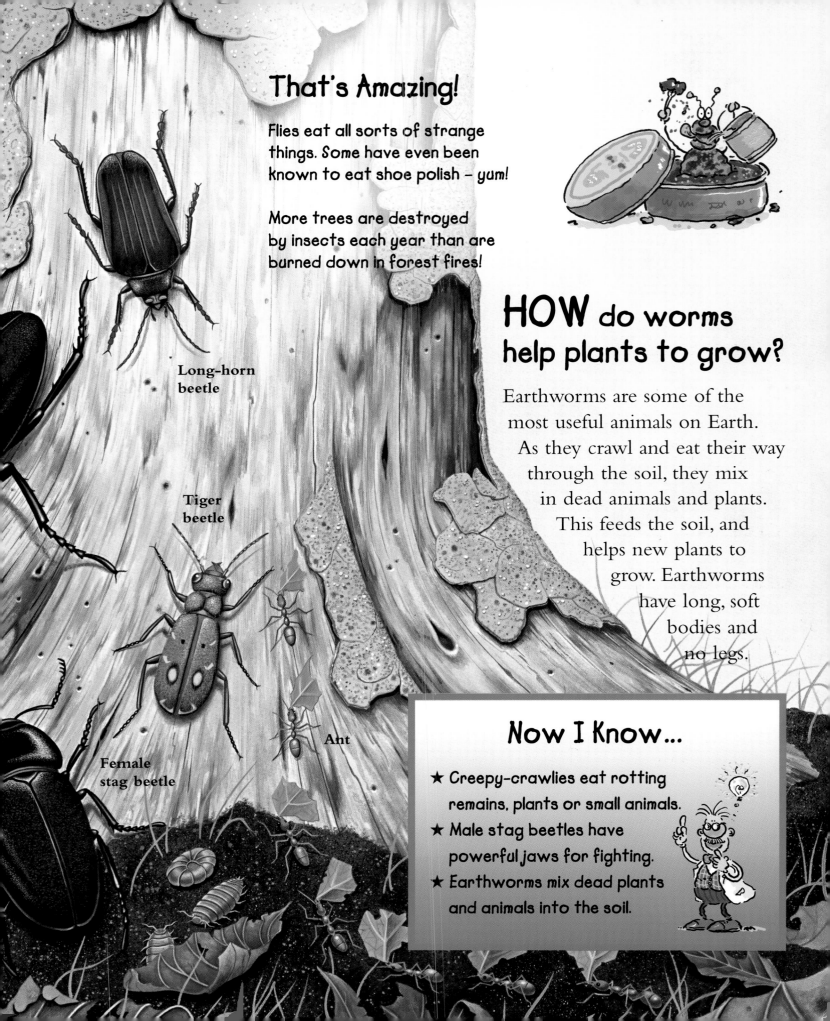

That's Amazing!

Flies eat all sorts of strange things. Some have even been known to eat shoe polish – yum!

More trees are destroyed by insects each year than are burned down in forest fires!

Long-horn beetle

Tiger beetle

Ant

Female stag beetle

HOW do worms help plants to grow?

Earthworms are some of the most useful animals on Earth. As they crawl and eat their way through the soil, they mix in dead animals and plants. This feeds the soil, and helps new plants to grow. Earthworms have long, soft bodies and no legs.

Now I Know...

★ Creepy-crawlies eat rotting remains, plants or small animals.
★ Male stag beetles have powerful jaws for fighting.
★ Earthworms mix dead plants and animals into the soil.

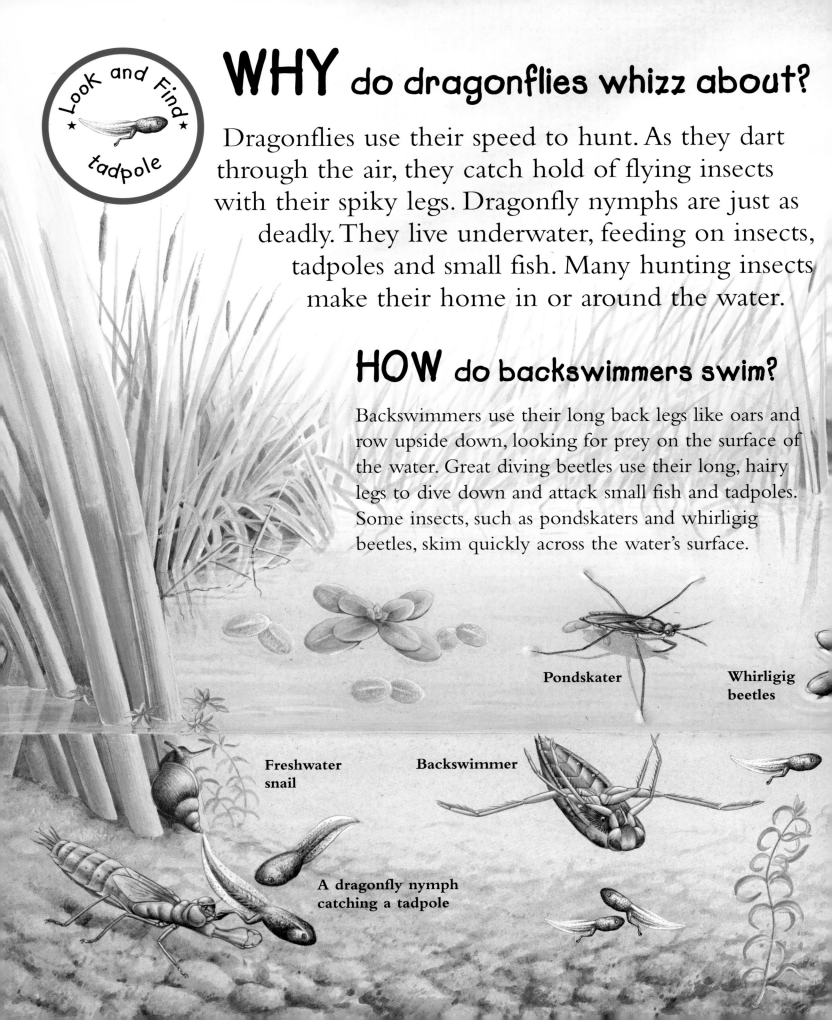

Look and Find
★ ★
tadpole

WHY do dragonflies whizz about?

Dragonflies use their speed to hunt. As they dart through the air, they catch hold of flying insects with their spiky legs. Dragonfly nymphs are just as deadly. They live underwater, feeding on insects, tadpoles and small fish. Many hunting insects make their home in or around the water.

HOW do backswimmers swim?

Backswimmers use their long back legs like oars and row upside down, looking for prey on the surface of the water. Great diving beetles use their long, hairy legs to dive down and attack small fish and tadpoles. Some insects, such as pondskaters and whirligig beetles, skim quickly across the water's surface.

Pondskater

Whirligig beetles

Freshwater snail

Backswimmer

A dragonfly nymph catching a tadpole

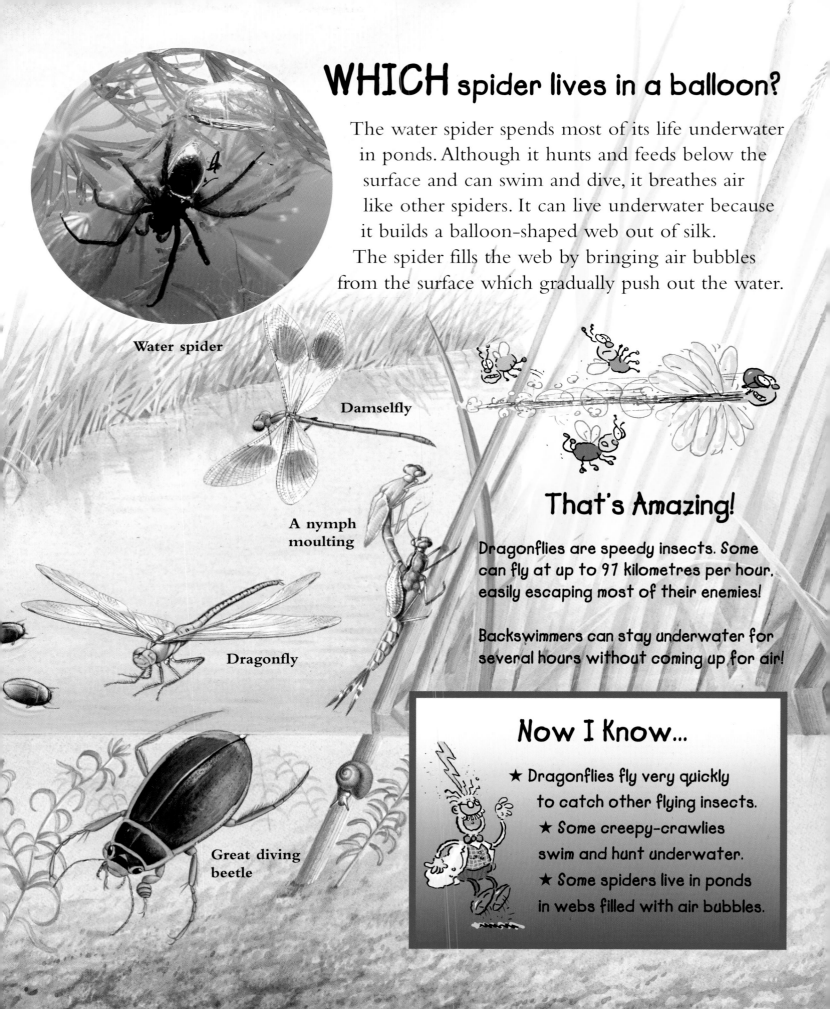

WHICH spider lives in a balloon?

The water spider spends most of its life underwater in ponds. Although it hunts and feeds below the surface and can swim and dive, it breathes air like other spiders. It can live underwater because it builds a balloon-shaped web out of silk. The spider fills the web by bringing air bubbles from the surface which gradually push out the water.

Water spider

Damselfly

A nymph moulting

Dragonfly

Great diving beetle

That's Amazing!

Dragonflies are speedy insects. Some can fly at up to 97 kilometres per hour, easily escaping most of their enemies!

Backswimmers can stay underwater for several hours without coming up for air!

Now I Know...

★ Dragonflies fly very quickly to catch other flying insects.
★ Some creepy-crawlies swim and hunt underwater.
★ Some spiders live in ponds in webs filled with air bubbles.

WHY do spiders spin webs?

Some spiders use sticky traps to help them catch food. They spin fine webs, using silk made in special glands in their bodies. The silk is liquid inside the spider, but hardens into a strong thread outside its body. When an insect becomes tangled in the web, the spider feels it struggling through hairs on its legs, and rushes over to kill it.

Garden cross spider

Web-spinning spiders never get caught in their own webs. They have special greasy feet that slip easily along the silk lines.

WHAT shape is an orb-web spider's web?

Orb-web spiders weave their round webs in open areas, often between tree branches or flower stems. Some spiders lie in wait close by for insects to get caught. Others hold a thread of silk, called a trap line, attached to the centre of the web, and hide nearby. When an insect lands in the web, the line vibrates and the spider darts out to attack it.

Some spiders wrap up their captured victims in silk, so they can't escape. Later, they return to the web to eat the insects.

That's Amazing!

Some spiders spin a new web every night. They are experts, so it takes only one hour!

Spider silk is thinner than a hair, but it is stronger than steel wire of the same thickness!

WHERE do some baby spiders live?

Some spiders do not spin webs to catch other animals, but use them instead as 'nurseries' to protect their young. The spiders guard their eggs until the tiny spiderlings are ready to spill out – usually after the babies' second moult. These webs are built in plants or shrubs.

Nursery web spider

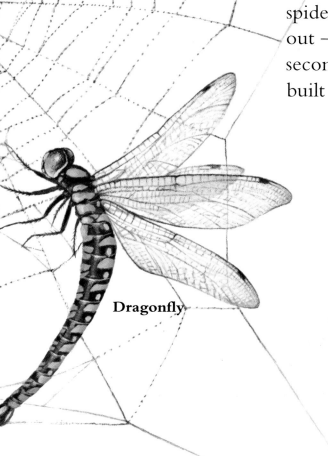

Dragonfly

Now I Know...

★ Spiders use their fine, sticky webs to capture their prey.
★ Orb-web spiders spin round webs made from silk.
★ Some spiders look after their young in 'nursery' webs.

17

Look and Find
★ ★
red mite

WHICH spiders are hunters?

Hunting spiders creep up or pounce on their prey as it passes by. Most hunters have excellent eyesight to help them spot their next meal from far away. Once the prey is captured, the spiders inject their victim with poison from their fangs, before wrapping it tightly in silk thread. The poison first kills the creature, then slowly turns its insides into a gooey soup, which the spiders suck up. Without the help of these skilful hunters, the world would be overrun with insects.

A trapdoor spider lies in wait for a passing cricket

That's Amazing!

Spiders have lived on Earth for 400 million years - they were around even before the first dinosaurs!

HOW do tarantulas catch their prey?

Tarantulas are the world's largest spiders, and live in rainforests in South America. They spend the day hiding in burrows and come out at night to hunt. Tarantulas have poor eyesight, but their legs are covered in fine hairs that pick up vibrations from moving animals.

A tarantula hunting

WHY do trapdoor spiders hide?

The trapdoor spider uses a clever trick to catch victims. After digging a burrow, it covers the hole with a lid and hides. As night falls, the spider lifts the trapdoor and waits. When a creature passes nearby, the spider feels the ground vibrate and leaps out. It stuns its victim with poison before dragging it into its burrow to devour it.

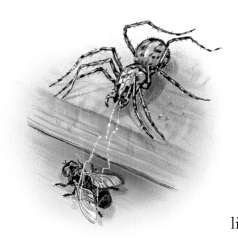

The bolas spider traps its prey in a cunning way. It uses special glands in its body to create a ball of sticky gum. Then it spins a line of silk, and attaches the ball to the end. The spider catches insects by swinging the line of silk like a lasso.

Cricket

Now I Know...

★ Hunting spiders don't catch prey in webs, but hunt on the ground or in trees.
★ Tarantulas have hairy legs to help them feel for dinner.
★ Trapdoor spiders hide underground to ambush prey.

19

WHICH insect looks like a twig?

All creepy-crawlies have enemies that want to eat them. Some stay alive by disguising themselves as something that isn't worth eating. Others blend cleverly into their **habitats**. Stick insects have bodies that look like twigs, while leaf insects look like bright green leaves. Some caterpillars even look like birds' droppings. Other creatures contain poison or bad-tasting chemicals that make them impossible to eat.

WHY does a mantis pray?

A mantis holds its front legs together while waiting to attack, so that it looks like it is praying. If an insect lands nearby, the mantis stays perfectly still, but keeps watch by swivelling its head slightly. Then it suddenly strikes. Its front legs snap around its victim and it begins to feed immediately. The mantis' stick-like green body blends into the surrounding leaves. This helps it to stay hidden from hungry enemies.

That's Amazing!

The bombardier beetle shoots its enemies with a cloud of hot, stinging liquid!

The longest insect is the tropical stick insect which reaches 35 cm!

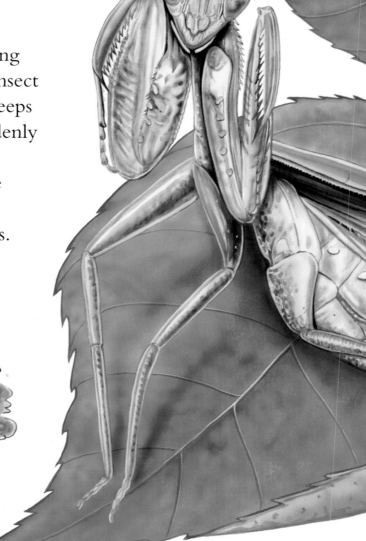

Praying mantis

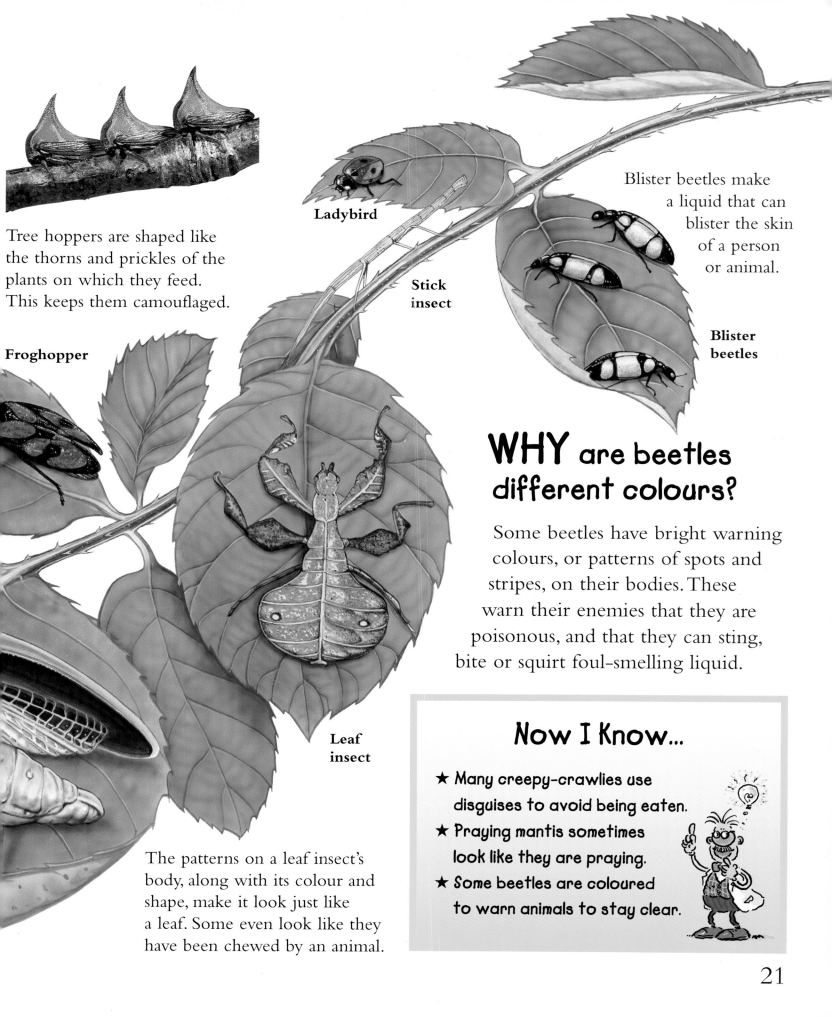

Tree hoppers are shaped like the thorns and prickles of the plants on which they feed. This keeps them camouflaged.

Ladybird

Froghopper

Stick insect

Blister beetles make a liquid that can blister the skin of a person or animal.

Blister beetles

Leaf insect

WHY are beetles different colours?

Some beetles have bright warning colours, or patterns of spots and stripes, on their bodies. These warn their enemies that they are poisonous, and that they can sting, bite or squirt foul-smelling liquid.

The patterns on a leaf insect's body, along with its colour and shape, make it look just like a leaf. Some even look like they have been chewed by an animal.

Now I Know...

★ Many creepy-crawlies use disguises to avoid being eaten.
★ Praying mantis sometimes look like they are praying.
★ Some beetles are coloured to warn animals to stay clear.

WHY are slugs slimy?

Slugs slither from place to place, carrying their bodies on a big block of muscle called a foot. The slime that pours from their bodies makes a slippery track that stops the foot from getting damaged as it scrapes across the ground. It also stops the slugs from drying out, even though they live in damp places. Snails are very like slugs, but have hard shells to protect their soft bodies.

That's Amazing!

The cone shell snail can inject a poison, strong enough to kill a human being, through its spear-like teeth!

The tongues of some sea snails are so strong they can drill through the shell of other animals!

Banded garden snail

Slug

HOW does a snail grow its shell?

A snail builds its own shell from a mineral called calcium carbonate. As the snail grows bigger, it adds more and more material to the spiral-shaped shell. When a snail is disturbed, or if the weather becomes very dry, it pulls itself back into its shell for protection.

Giant African snail

WHERE are a snail's eyes?

Snails have eyes on the tip of two long feelers called **tentacles**. A snail has two pairs of tentacles on its head. One pair is shorter than the other. The eyes are on the longer pair, while the shorter pair are used by the snail for smelling and feeling its way around.

Now I Know...

★ The slime made by a slug helps its foot to slide across the ground.

★ Snails build shells to protect their soft bodies.

★ A snail's eyes are on the end of long tentacles.

WHY do ants live together?

★ Look and Find ★
spider

Ants are social insects, like bees and termites. They live and work together in large, organized groups called **colonies**. Each nest contains a single queen, which lays all the eggs. Most of the other ants are female workers. They build the home, search for food, keep the nest clean, fight enemies and look after the young **larvae**.

Termites are amazing colony builders. They make mud nests up to four times the height of an adult human.

Wood ants in their nest

Larvae

That's Amazing!

When ants find food, they mark a smelly trail to their nest, so others can follow!

Tiny ants can lift objects more than 20 times their own weight!

24

WHICH ants are like storage jars?

Honeypot ants use certain worker ants as 'storage jars' to hold plant juices. In the summer when food is plentiful, these ants are fed nectar and honeydew by the other workers. They swell up like balloons, and hang upside down in the nest. When food supplies are low, the workers tap them with their antennae to make them release food.

Honeypot ants

HOW do ants make their tree-top tents?

Weaver ants 'sew' leaves together to make tents in the tree-tops, using their young like a needle and thread. Each ant holds a larva in its mouth, and pokes it against the edges of the leaves. The larva makes a sticky thread that binds the leaves together.

Weaver ants

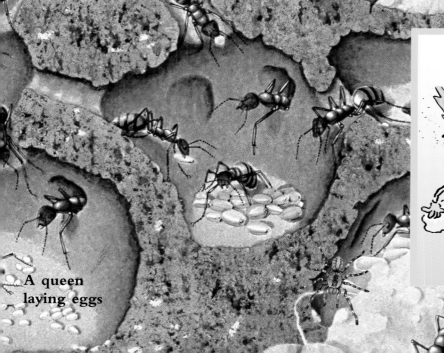

Female worker ants searching for food

Now I Know...

★ The queen ant is the most important member of the nest.
★ Some honeypot ants store tasty food in their bodies.
★ Weaver ants use their larva like a needle and thread.

A queen laying eggs

25

Look and Find
★ ★
butterfly

WHY do honeybees like flowers?

In summer, honeybees buzz busily from flower to flower – feeding on sweet nectar and pollen grains. Back at their nest or hive, they turn the nectar into honey and make 'pollen bread', which they store in wax honeycombs. When a honeybee finds a new source of food, it flies home and performs a special 'dance' to tell the other bees where to find it. The closer the food is, the faster and faster the bee dances.

HOW do bees carry pollen?

As bees eat nectar, they rub against tiny yellow pollen grains made by the flower. This yellow powder gets caught on their bodies and the bees comb it into hairy baskets on their back legs. They then carry the pollen back to the nest. During their food-gathering flights, bees spread pollen from one flower to another. This is called **pollination**.

A honeybee collecting nectar

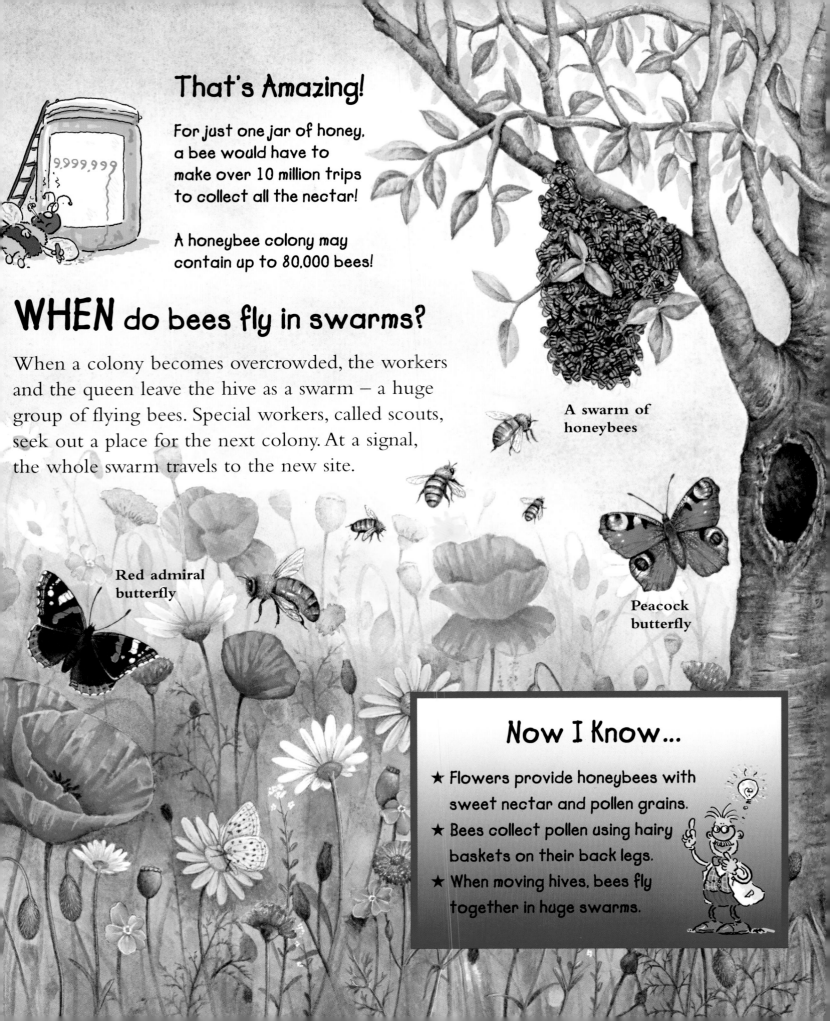

That's Amazing!

For just one jar of honey, a bee would have to make over 10 million trips to collect all the nectar!

A honeybee colony may contain up to 80,000 bees!

WHEN do bees fly in swarms?

When a colony becomes overcrowded, the workers and the queen leave the hive as a swarm – a huge group of flying bees. Special workers, called scouts, seek out a place for the next colony. At a signal, the whole swarm travels to the new site.

A swarm of honeybees

Red admiral butterfly

Peacock butterfly

Now I Know...

★ Flowers provide honeybees with sweet nectar and pollen grains.
★ Bees collect pollen using hairy baskets on their back legs.
★ When moving hives, bees fly together in huge swarms.

Look and Find ★ snail

WHY do glow-worms glow?

Glow-worms are not actually worms, but small beetles. To attract a mate, the females give out a bright light made by chemicals in an organ on the underside of their abdomens. Female glow-worms have no wings and have to climb to the top of blades of grass to signal to flying males. Fireflies are close relatives of glow-worms. Both male and female give out a yellowish glow.

WHY do grasshoppers 'sing'?

Grasshoppers use sound to attract mates and warn rivals. The males 'sing' by scraping their back legs against a vein in their front wings, like a violin player drawing a bow across a string. Each species has its own special tune.

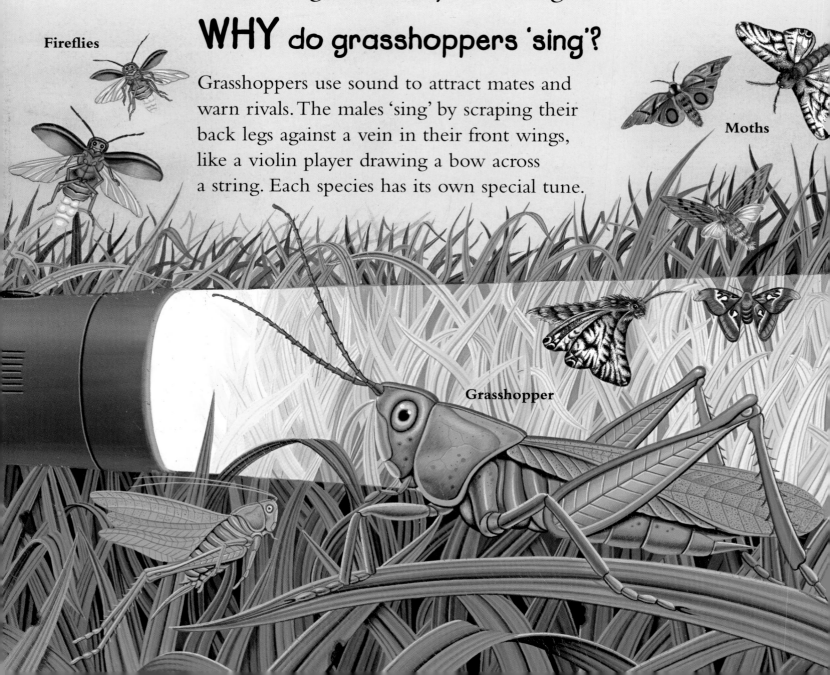

Fireflies

Moths

Grasshopper

WHICH insect is noisiest?

The noisiest insect in the world is the cicada. Males spend a lot of time in trees where they 'chirrup' loudly using two plates on the side of their abdomen. They can be heard over 400 metres away – about the distance of four football pitches.

That's Amazing!

A South American firefly, the railway worm, got its name because it flashes red and green like a railway signal!

Some insects hear sounds using the delicate hairs on their antennae!

Summer nights are filled with all kinds of insects sending messages to each other using light and sound.

Snail

Female glow-worms

Now I Know...

★ Glow-worms and fireflies send messages to each other using glowing light.
★ Grasshoppers 'sing' to attract mates or warn rivals.
★ Male cicadas are the noisiest insects – ever!

CREEPY-CRAWLY QUIZ

What have you remembered about creepy-crawlies? Test your knowledge and see how much you have learned.

1 What sort of animal is a ladybird?
a) spider
b) mollusc
c) insect

2 What do butterflies eat?
a) nectar
b) other insects
c) honey

3 Where do grasshoppers lay their eggs?
a) in a pond
b) in the air
c) underground

4 Which creepy-crawlies fly?
a) spiders
b) dragonflies
c) slugs

5 From what is a spider's web made?
a) plants
b) wood
c) silk

6 Which creepy-crawly has a shell on its back?
a) earthworm
b) slug
c) snail

7 Which sort of ant lays eggs?
a) queen
b) worker
c) larva

8 Which of these creepy-crawlies can swim?
a) earthworm
b) adult dragonfly
c) water spider

9 What do tree hoppers look like?
a) leaves
b) thorns
c) sticks

10 Which creepy-crawly is the noisiest?
a) slug
b) cicada
c) bee

Find the answers on page 32.

GLOSSARY

abdomen The lower part of an insect that contains the stomach, and in females produces the eggs.

antennae The sensitive 'feelers' on the head of an insect that are used to touch, taste or smell.

arachnids The group of animals with eight legs, such as spiders and scorpions.

colonies Groups of the same type of animal, such as ants and honeybees, that live and work together.

compound eyes The type of eyes found in many insects. Each eye is made up of thousands of tiny lenses packed together.

exoskeleton The outer skeleton of an insect or spider that supports and protects the rest of the body.

habitats The natural homes of animals or plants.

insects The group of animals that have six legs and three body sections.

invertebrates The group of animals, such as insects and molluscs, without a backbone.

larvae The young of an insect.

metamorphosis When a larva, such as a caterpillar, completely changes its body as it turns into an adult.

molluscs The group of animals, such as slugs and snails, that have soft bodies. Most molluscs' bodies are protected with hard outer shells.

moulting When an insect or spider sheds its outer skin before growing into its new one.

nectar The sweet liquid produced by flowers, and eaten by bees and other insects.

nymphs Young insects, such as young grasshoppers, that look like tiny copies of their parents.

pollination The transfer of pollen by animals or the wind between flowers.

prey An animal that is hunted or killed by another animal.

pupae The stage during metamorphosis when young insects change into adults.

species A particular type of animal or plant.

spiderlings Young spiders.

tentacles On a snail, the long stalks that contain the eyes.

thorax The middle section of an insect that contains the legs and sometimes the wings.

tracheae The tiny breathing tubes in an insect.

INDEX

Answers to the Creepy-crawly Quiz

★ 1 c ★ 2 a ★ 3 c ★ 4 b ★ 5 c ★ 6 c ★ 7 a ★ 8 c ★ 9 b ★ 10 b